A Book of Children's Rhymes

A Book of Children's Rhymes

Pixie Dean

Illustrations by Jackie at KJA Artists

Copyright © 2015 Pixie Dean

The moral right of the author has been asserted.

Apart from any fair dealing for the purposes of research or private study, or criticism or review, as permitted under the Copyright, Designs and Patents Act 1988, this publication may only be reproduced, stored or transmitted, in any form or by any means, with the prior permission in writing of the publishers, or in the case of reprographic reproduction in accordance with the terms of licences issued by the Copyright Licensing Agency. Enquiries concerning reproduction outside those terms should be sent to the publishers.

Matador
9 Priory Business Park,
Wistow Road, Kibworth Beauchamp,
Leicestershire. LE8 0RX
Tel: 0116 279 2299
Email: books@troubador.co.uk
Web: www.troubador.co.uk/matador
Twitter: @matadorbooks

ISBN 978 1784625 078
British Library Cataloguing in Publication Data.
A catalogue record for this book is available from the British Library.

Printed and bound in Malta by Gutenberg Press Ltd.
Typeset in 14pt Baskerville by Troubador Publishing Ltd, Leicester, UK

Matador is an imprint of Troubador Publishing Ltd

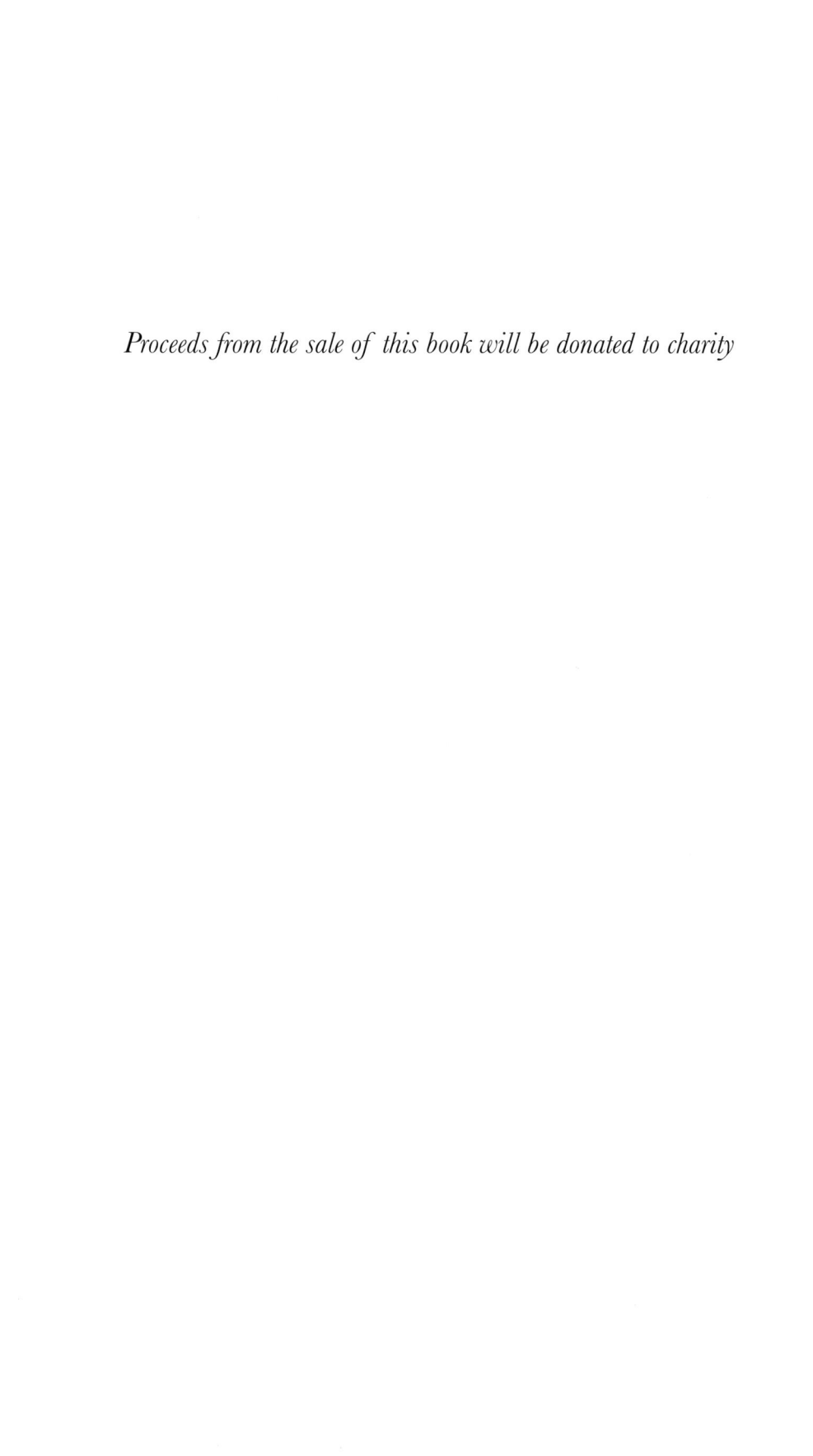

Proceeds from the sale of this book will be donated to charity

Contents

Gypsy Rosie Lee	1
Limerick – Baa Baa Black Sheep	4
A Street Full of Candy	5
Limerick – A Man from Bombay	8
I had a Tyrannosaurus	9
Limerick – A Man called Mark	13
The Little Fatty Man	14
The Magic Blue Stone	18
Limerick – Plastic	26
Mary, Mary	27
Paul and the Disappearing Ball	28
The Owl and the Pussycat	31
Horace Shakespeare	32
Limerick – Chewing Gum	35

Limerick – A Swimmer called Pete	36
The Little Dancing Pig	37
Limerick – Yvonne	43
Hey Diddle Diddle	44
The Chase	45
Two Little Dickie Birds	48
The Computer Whizz-kid	49
Limerick – A Toad	52
I Want to See the Sea	53
PC Plod	57
Waiter, Waiter	59
Strange Goings-on in the Street	60
Limerick – There once was a man from Surrey	63
'Twas the Night Before Christmas	64

Jack Sprat	70
Limerick – Old Mother Hubbard	71
Postman – No pat!	72
Limerick – Eskimo	76
Miriam the Mouse	77
Limerick – Fog	84
Little Miss Muffet	85
The Hungry Caterpillar	86
Megan & Macy	89
Sophie Wilson	94
Icky Wicky Woo	99
The Loch Ness Monster	101
Lulu Letterbox	106
Acknowledgements	113

Gypsy Rosie Lee

A woman known as Rosie Lee
Was an ultra cunning lass, you see
She read people's palms and crystal balls
Wore gold hooped earrings and a shawl

But what the folk didn't realise
They were being conned – *I have my spies!*
You see we followed Rosie Lee
And no true gypsy blood had she
She didn't have some special power
For each night she worked and by the hour
At a fish shop serving chips
Mushy peas and curried dips.

Then throughout the day she sat in a tent
Where gullible people would frequent
And that's how we knew she was a crook
Her fortune-telling came from a book!

She had it on her lap while she
Professed the future she could see
She donned a wig and folded scarf
Did she tell porkies? Oooooh not half!

She told each soul all kinds of dross
But Rosie didn't give a toss!
It was all made up of course – not true
And thus earned herself a bob or two
She told them fibs and nonsense 'til the
Customers crossed her palms with silver!
Now that's the bit that is not funny
As she was swindling them out of money
She was just a cheat for all to see
Not a genuine fortune-teller gypsy
So, if ever you are so inclined
And one day you are sat behind
A table with a crystal ball
Be careful that you do not fall
Under the gypsy's magic spell
Especially if there's a fish shop smell!

Limerick

Baa baa black sheep have you lost your fleece?
Yes sir, yes sir, let's call the police
Then we'll tell the master
And we'll also tell the dame
That a wolf in a sheep's clothing could be lurking down the lane!!!

A Street Full of Candy

The children were playing on the village green
Then down from the sky, something n'er before seen!
All kinds of candy falling like rain
Millions and trillions of sweets – 'twas insane!
Sherberts, fizzy jellies, gold chocolate coins galore
Squishy pink mallows, lollipops and more

Bright coloured jelly beans like jewels from a crown
Fruit drops and bonbons all spilling down
On to the faces, around children's feet
So much yummy candy it filled up the street.

Fruit bursting colours, like a rainbow of light
A street full of sweets was a marvellous sight
The village resembled a jewel-filled sea
And more to the point the sweets were all *free*!

The children were shrieking with squeals of delight
As the sweets rained down all day and all night
Never, not ever, had this happened before
Chocolate and candy piled high as a door!

But alas the next morning the *real* rain appeared
And it was torrential and fierce and the children all feared
That all of their candy would be swept away by the rain
And it was true… rivers of sweets were washed
down the drain

All the young smiley faces turned to pitiable sorrow
Every last sweet would be gone by tomorrow
The sweet filled streets would soon be forgotten
But at least all those children's teeth won't be rotten!

Limerick

There once was a man from Bombay
Whose hair was receding each day
He didn't want to look old
And worse, end up bald
So he sported a bright pink toupee!

I had a Tyrannosaurus

I had a tyrannosaurus, I kept him in a shed
I created him with DNA and brought him back from dead
This creature's recognition was known from far and wide
I knew my tyrannosaurus was going to be difficult to hide

He roared to life quite quickly and to my horror and surprise
Whilst he had most of his features, he had no tyrannosaurus eyes
He gladly wasn't affected by depression or the dumps
Nor tyrannosaurus measles or tyrannosaurus mumps

I'd brought him back from Neverland but sadly he was blind
But he was such an awesome creature that I really didn't mind!
I called him George the Juggernaut, he bumped into posts and gates
He crashed into cars and lorries and he trod on all my plates

I fastened on a lead rein and led him through the streets
And all the children patted him and gave him chewy sweets
He had a fearsome structure and a thousand razor teeth
He had fire in his belly but he was a softie underneath

My father though, regarded him with terror in his eyes
He didn't want a colony of tyrannosaurusi
He borrowed a machine gun from a friend called Wallace Mitty
And showed my tyrannosaurus no tyrannosaurus-pity!

No longer now he gambols in the orchard in the rain
No longer can I lead him through the village 'ere again
No longer in the morning does the neighbourhood rejoice
To the triumphantly, tymphanic tyrannosaurus voice

So I miss my mighty monster as I go about my chores
I miss his giant thudding and his nightly scary roars
I had a tyrannosaurus and I'm sad that he is gone
And I've no more DNA left to make another one!

Limerick

There once was a man called Mark
Who went sailing one night in the dark
He fell off his boat
And was grabbed by the throat
Then swallowed by a killer white shark!

The Little Fatty Man

A man considered somewhat batty
Five feet tall but rather fatty
Because of his huge size and weight
Got wedged between his garden gate

The neighbours soon they all appeared
But stuck fast was he they all now feared!
Tried as they might to push and shove
They even prayed for help above!
They tugged him, pulled him, but not an inch
Some suggested they hire a winch!
Others cried, 'Let's try some grease'
Another yelled, 'Call the Police!'

The hours passed and nighttime fell
The man began to scream and yell
Then a woman had a scheme
It wasn't as daft as it first seemed!
She sprinkled pepper on his clothes
In his hair and up his nose
Then in a jiff, a whopping SNEEZE!
The man flew out just like a breeze!

He landed on the neighbour's shed
Slid down the roof and banged his head
Then slipped into an open drain
And was never to be seen again!

The Magic Blue Stone

Jack was lying upon his bed
He put down the book he often read
He looked toward the sky ink-blue
As the strangest thing came into view
A peculiar shape of burning light
A glowing awesome blinding white

It was the brightest light Jack had seen
Then it slowly turned to vivid green!
Then coloured smoke and little stars
And behold appeared a man from Mars!
Who stood upon Jack's comfy bed
In astonishment Jack scratched his head!

A man, a mere few inches tall!
Who stretched out from a tiny ball
His skin was like a greenish leather
Then he rubbed his tiny hands together
More stars appeared then a whitish mist
And something unfurled out of his fist
It hovered freely in mid-air
The bluest stone seen anywhere!

The little man said of the stone,
'It has mystical powers – some still unknown!
Three wishes it will grant to you
This stone will make them all come true!
Its magic is beyond compare
So make your wishes if you dare
Three wishes and the magic will be spun
More than three and the magic spell will be undone!'
So little Jack climbed out of bed
And again he scratched his puzzled head
He held the stone up to the sky
'Oh magic stone, I wish that I could fly!'

A big *flash* then Jack soared up toward the ceiling
Zooming round his bed he rode – it was such a lovely feeling
He flew down towards the kitchen and out of the back door
He flew around the garden then down the street he tore
He felt free and was soaring like a bird
The fact that he was flying was really quite absurd
Rooftops and brick chimneys he skimmed with sheer delight
Cars looked like little ants from his elevated height

He still held the magic blue stone tightly in his hand
So he made a wish to be taken to a far off foreign land
Another *flash* and *bang* and he was there
With funny looking people and strange animals everywhere
They spoke a language he did not recognise
Orange and blue elephants walked before his eyes!
Red koala bears, turquoise tigers and lime kangaroos
Green spotted swans, tangerine geese and crimson cockatoos
He'd no idea at all where this funny place could be
But all Jack knew he felt such joy at being so carefree

He was feeling rather tired now and hungry for a snack
So wish number three was granted then, like magic,
a brown sack!
Full of creamy chocolates, multicoloured bags of sweets
Caramels and toffees and all other yummy treats!
He scoffed half the contents of the giant sweet-filled sack

And then, the rather worse for wear, pot-bellied greedy Jack
Was ready for a nice cool refreshing drink
So he made wish number *four*! – and he just didn't think!
'Oh no!' cried Jack, 'What have I done?
The magic now will be undone!'
And suddenly there was a flash of red
And little Jack was back in his bed
He felt dizzy, shaken and very tired
His exciting adventure had now expired
He fell back to sleep and pledged to himself as he was yawning
Not to tell a soul about his mysterious trip when he woke
the next morning!

Limerick

There are so many uses for plastic
Credit cards, coat hangers and Mastic
Electric cables and phones
Catseyes, traffic cones
The invention was simply fantastic!

Mary, Mary

Mary, Mary quite contrary
How does your garden grow?
With no flowers in the bed
And the lawn looking dead
I'd hazard a guess – pretty slow!

Paul and the Disappearing Ball

A little boy whose name was Paul
Was one day playing with a ball
It bounced so high and like a kite
It flew so high then out of sight

Paul wondered where the ball could be
So off he set to climb a tree
But the tree was of a beanstalk size
And up Paul climbed into the skies
He climbed through the sun and rain and snow
How far would his climbing go?
Then suddenly a land appeared
With a kindly man who had a beard
With cherubs, harps and softly clouds
And people meandering around in crowds
All with friendly smiley faces
There were pearly gates and white staircases
Then lo! Angels! – He counted seven!
Then realised he'd climbed to heaven

So shocked was he, he slipped and fell
And prayed he didn't land in hell
He fell down and down then back on land
Beside the tree with ball in hand!

The Owl and the Pussycat

The Owl and the Pussycat went to sea
On a beautiful luxury yacht
Said Owl to Pussycat
'As well as the money
You've forgotten the passports, you clot!'

Horace Shakespeare

Born Horace Shakespeare, a little boy
Who yearned not for a single toy
But demanded only pen and ink
With paper and a room to think
And from henceforth he did compose
Profound, prolific, pensive prose

But all was at a loss how he
Could pen such verse of quality
But alas it seemed his gift was fated
As to the Great Bard he was related!
Of Will Shakespeare's line there was but a dozen
And Horace was a distant cousin!
'Tis strange how genes will oft come out
A poetic talent he had no doubt
So, after growing up deprived and poor
With bailiffs knocking at his door
He got his writing into print
And swiftly made himself a mint
As all his work was quick to sell
And so of course… All's well that ends well!

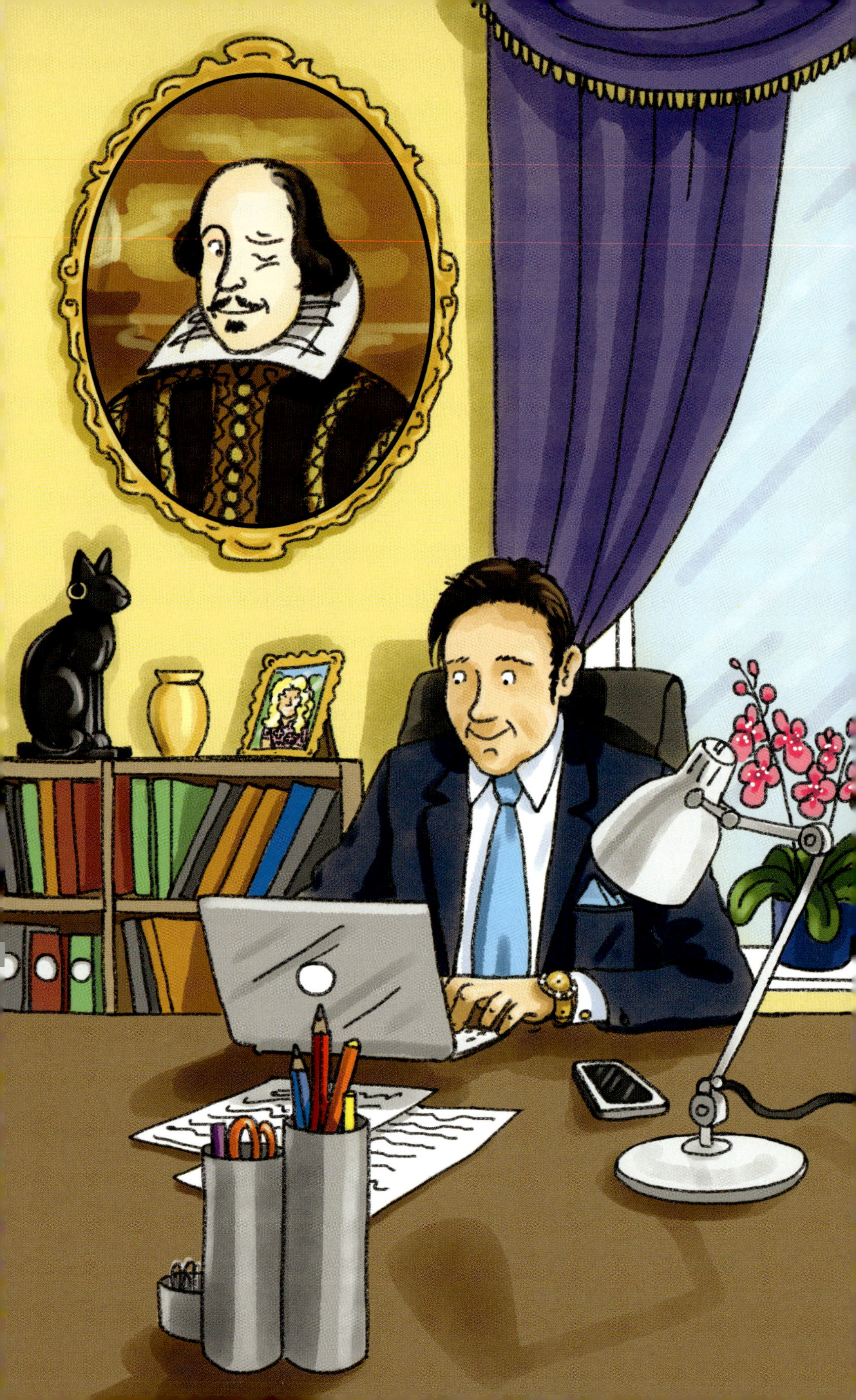

Limerick

Now this might seem quite odd to some
But a man who loved chewing gum
Used to swallow it too
Then one day went to the loo
And the toilet seat stuck to his bum!

Limerick

A brilliant swimmer called Pete
Loved nothing better than to compete
He always won every race
No one could keep up the pace
But then he did have size *sixteen feet*!

The Little Dancing Pig

It was market day and in the village square
The villagers all gathered 'round to stare
Whilst a band played a lively little jig
There in the centre performed a little dancing pig!!!

Clad in a scarlet spotted dainty skirt
And matching flowered frilly shirt
The little pig pirouetted like a ballerina
On her pointy little toes she twirled – you should have seen her!

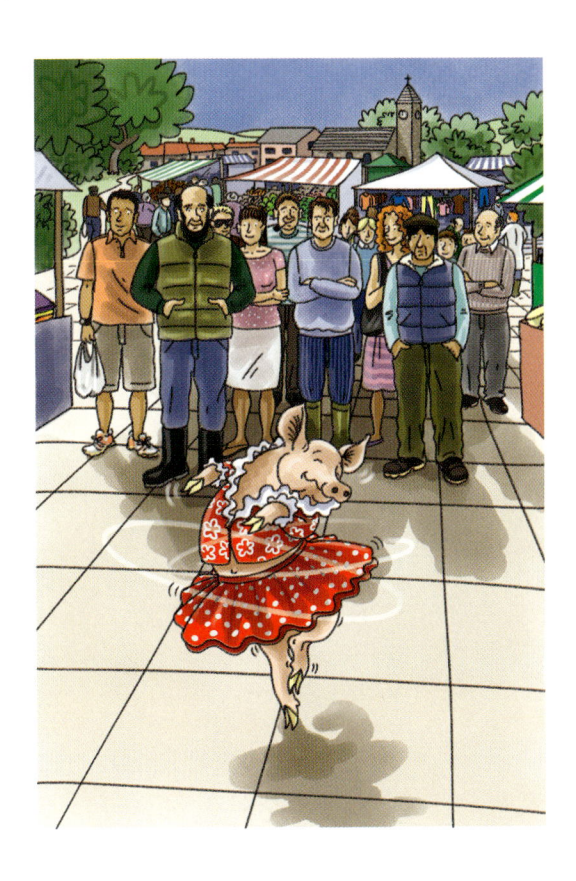

The crowd all cheered and shouted out for more
So the little pig obliged with an encore
The dancing pig squealed with sheer delight
As she whirled and spun and turned just like a kite

Then out of the blue appeared an angry looking farmer
The crowd all gasped for fear that he would harm her
He bent down and grabbed piggy by the tail
And yelled out, 'This naughty little pig is now for sale!'

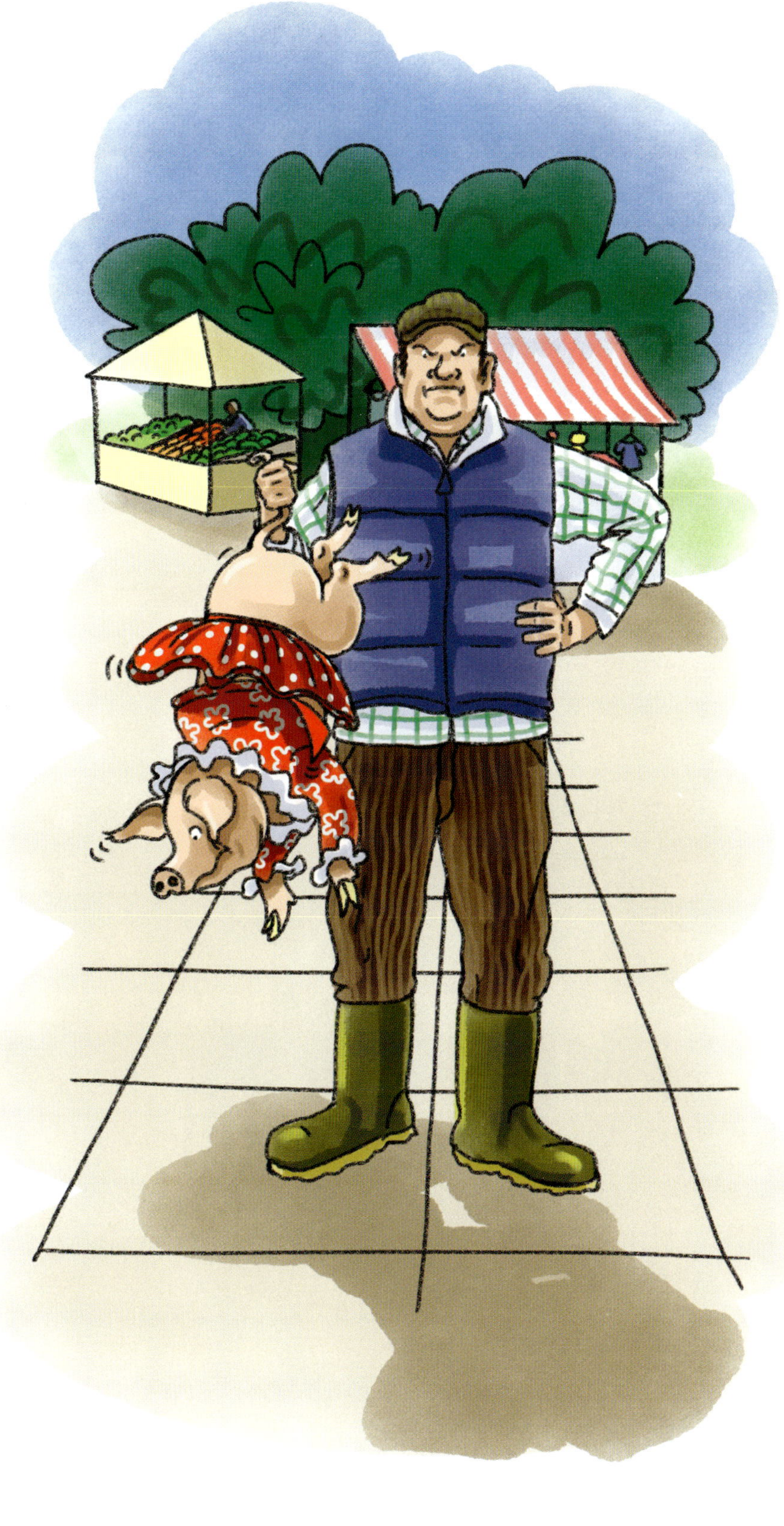

'For six months now I've tried to fatten her to sell
But she's a troublesome one, as you can clearly tell,
So I've had enough and now I'm wanting rid
So who'll be kind enough to offer me a bid?'

A man shouted, 'I'll buy and take her off you'
Another shouted, 'I too will bid, for I would like her too'
Then dozens of people all shouting from the crowd
It was chaos as everyone was calling out too loud

Then one little boy walked up to the pig and said
'You are the sweetest thing,' and stroked her silken head
'But I don't want you to be eaten at our table
You can live in our paddock and take shelter in our stable.'

'We have an orchard and you can eat apples all day long
And dance as often as you wish to the sound of the birdsong
And in the mud pond you can wallow – you will be happy this I know
But only if your owner is happy to let you go.'

The farmer's heart was melted and he readily agreed
The sale to this little boy was thereby guaranteed
'Take her son – I know she'll have a healthy life with you,'
And the little pig danced down the street for she was happy too!

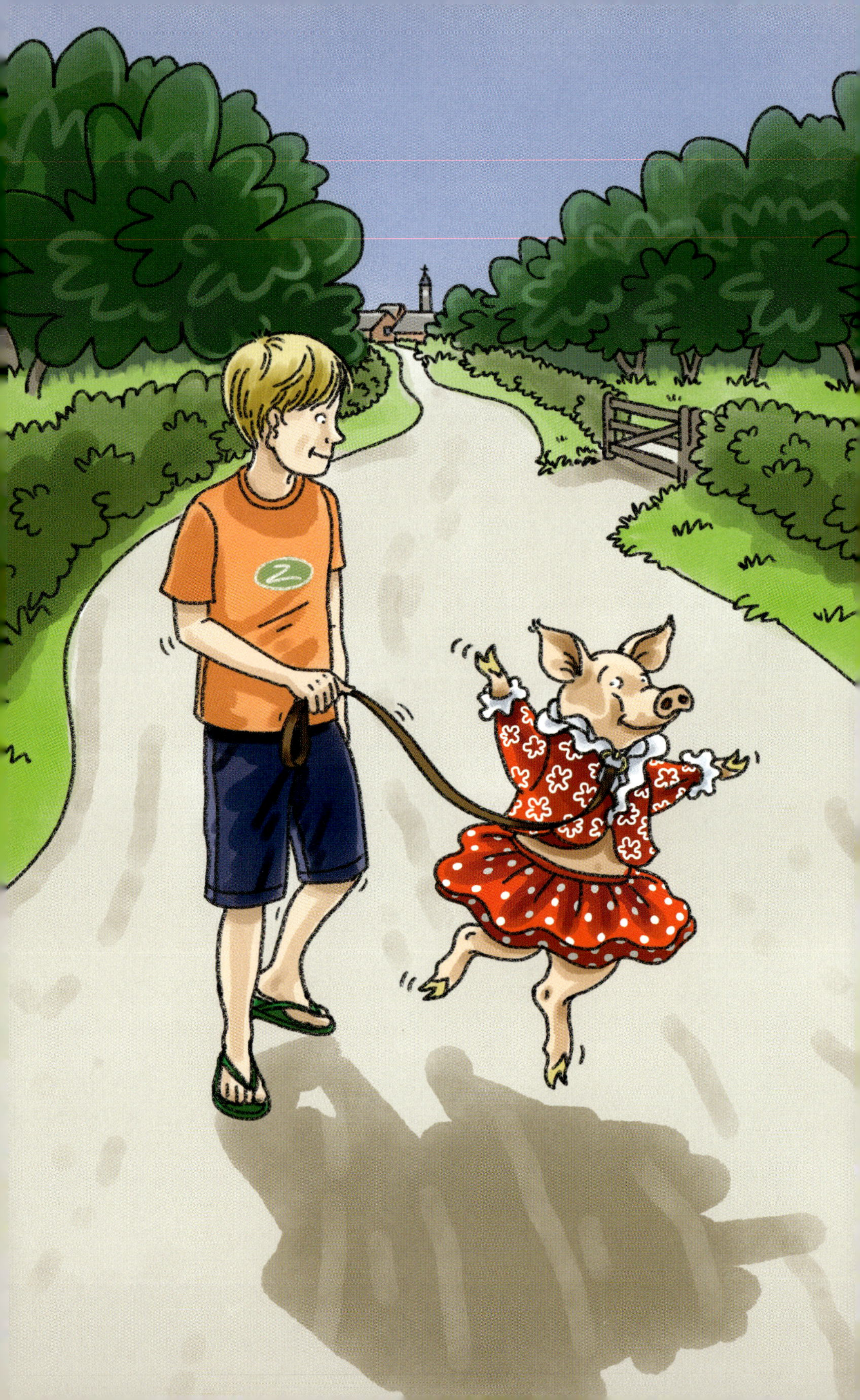

Limerick

There once was a girl called Yvonne
When she went to switch her TV on
It blew up in her face
And she was hurled into space
And she came down on a roof in Saigon!

Hey Diddle Diddle

Hey diddle diddle
The cat and the fiddle
The cow jumped over the moon
The cat and the fiddle
Fell out because
The fiddle couldn't play any tune!

The Chase

Bright was the moon that night
The snapping of a twig gave fright
Crisp were the leaves where I stood
Trodden on, they cracked like wood

Black was the sky full of mist
In fear, my hands clenched into fists
Hunched were the trees so tall
Owls out through the night did call

Held tight was my body numb
Tried squealing but my voice struck dumb
Held aghast by that horrific sight
As it slowly prowled the land that night

It groped its way slowly through the trees
As I stood there trembling at the knees
It manoeuvred stealthily like a snake
I begged my legs to run and make the break

I lifted one and then the other followed
My breath caught tight but then I finally swallowed
I was crashing into the things I could not see
Who made this night of black that blinded me?

With pounding heart and burning face afire
To seek refuge now was solely my desire
To turn back would surely be my death
I ran on, my chest was drained and dried of breath

By now my jellied legs could run no more
A protruding rock tripped me to the floor
And as I did I turned to face the scare
That ghastly creature – but lo, it was not there!

Relieved that I was wholly granted free
The exit from the thing t'was chasing me
My body drenched in sweat with ruffled hair
I woke up from yet another bad nightmare!

Two Little Dickie Birds

Two little dickie birds sitting on a wall
One was fat and one was small
Fly away Peter, fly away Paul,
Come back thinner, come back tall!

The Computer Whizz-kid

On his computer every week
A boy was nicknamed Techno Freak
Such an IT expert was he
He slept beside his own PC
Every minute of the day
Hours and hours he'd tap away

Some would think him rather sad
Others thought he might be mad
So-called friends would point and smirk
Because he loved his IT work
But while these children had their fun
He secretly knew that he had won
For unbeknown to them he had
Done something special for a lad
For whilst friends played and called him names
He'd been inventing computer games
Not one, alas but twenty-two
And snapped up by manufacturers who
Made him famous overnight
So much so his future's bright
It earned him millions in the bank
When his friends heard their hearts all sank
And each one in turn then did pretend
To be of course his loyal friend

But he could see right through their scam
And politely told them all to scram
The essence of this rhyme is thus
Don't disrespect a genius!

Limerick

There once was a daring young toad
Who ventured to cross over the road
He leapt out too fast
When a cyclist whizzed past
And now he walks pigeon-toed!

I Want to See the Sea!

I want to see the sea
How much further have we got?
This car is getting very hot
I've no more sweets – I ate the lot!
I want to see the sea!

I want to see the sea
Don't want more silly games to play
I've been cooped up in this car all day
Let me on the beach to play
I want to see the sea!

I want to see the sea
Dad's 'kiss me quick' hat on my head
To stop my face from burning red
Mum stretched out on her sun bed
I want to see the sea!

I want to see the sea
Cool ice lollies down my throat
Building sand castles with a moat
Watching people lose their float
I want to see the sea!

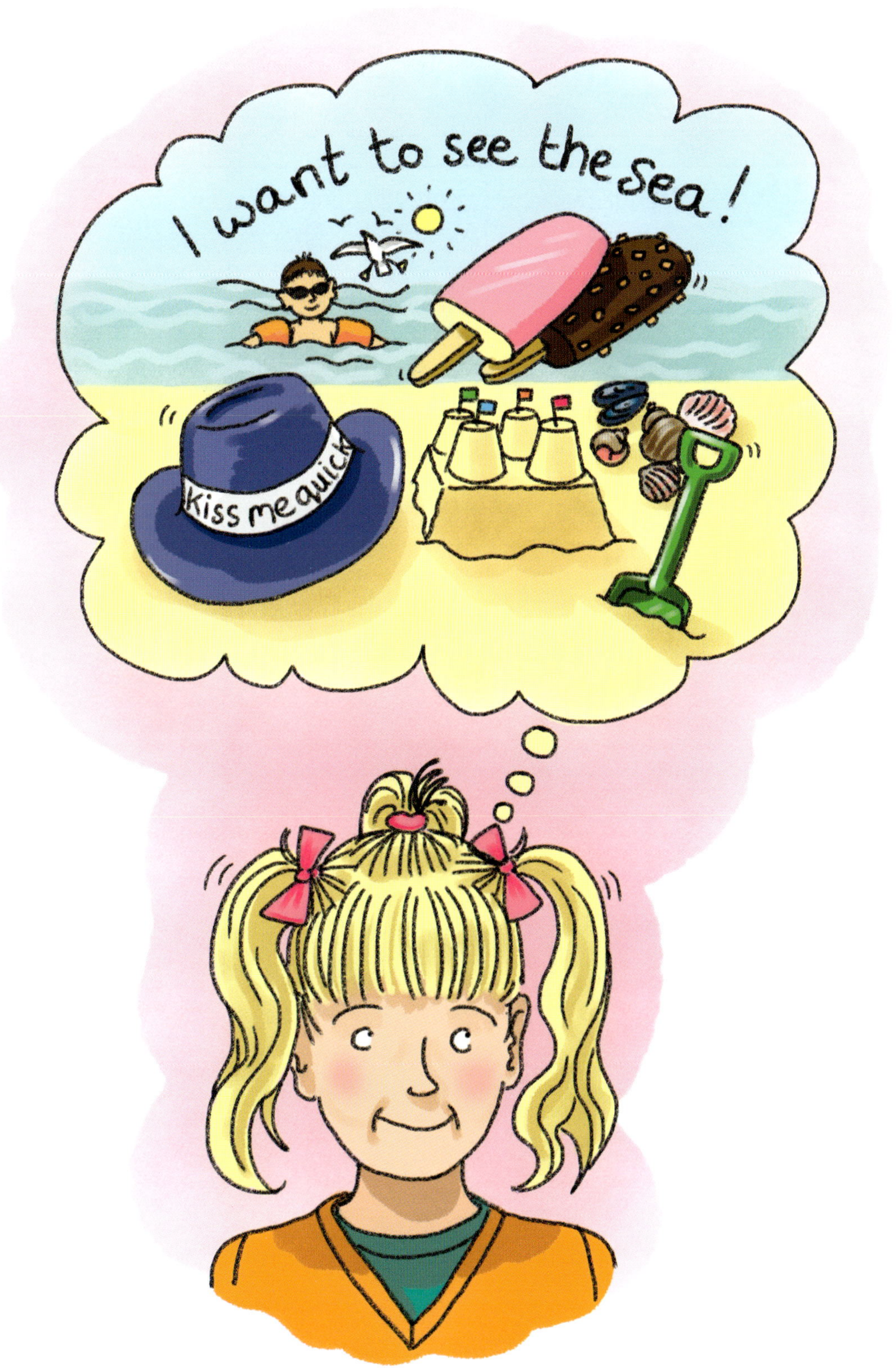
I want to see the sea!
Kiss me quick

I want to see the sea
Donkeys running across the sands
People topping up their tans
Children swimming with arm-bands
I want to see the sea!

I want to see the sea
Collecting sea shells on my spade
Rinsing them with lemonade
Dad asleep half in the shade
I want to see the sea!

I want to see the sea
But then there is a *bang* and *jolt*!
The car comes to a juddering halt
Dad declares a mechanical fault
No sea you see for me!

PC Plod

The villagers all called him Plod
A snail-like, rotund, dozy clod
And for an officer of the Law
He was not a good ambassador
Flabby belly, crumpled hat
Short on stature, hugely fat
He looks not like a policeman should
Too much beer and too much pud!

What good would he be on a chase?
With leaden legs and reddened face
He is supposed to be the *'thin'* blue line
I won't be dialling 999!

Waiter, Waiter

Dear Waiter, I don't want to seem rude
But I really can't consume this food!
My steak is so rare
I nearly fell of my chair
Because a minute ago it just mooed!

Strange Goings-on in the Street

My gran lives in a nearby street
Of picket fences, gardens neat
A place of peacefulness and charm
No thugs to do one any harm
But during each cold winter's night
There's to be seen the oddest sight
Apparently whilst folk all sleep
From shed doors some objects creep
Lawnmowers, rollers, forks and spades
Hedge cutters, shears with rusty blades
Plant pots, trowels and bags of peat
All dancing down this low lit street
So I went to witness with my own eyes
From my gran's garden in disguise
And sure enough when all was dark
No sound of sparrow or the lark
Just the moon and tooting owl
And then… the things were on the prowl
All shed doors opened and out they rolled
Into the street so deathly cold
And they gave each other a warm embrace
With a glowing smile upon their face
And I watched them joyfully as they danced
Twirling, reeling – I was entranced!

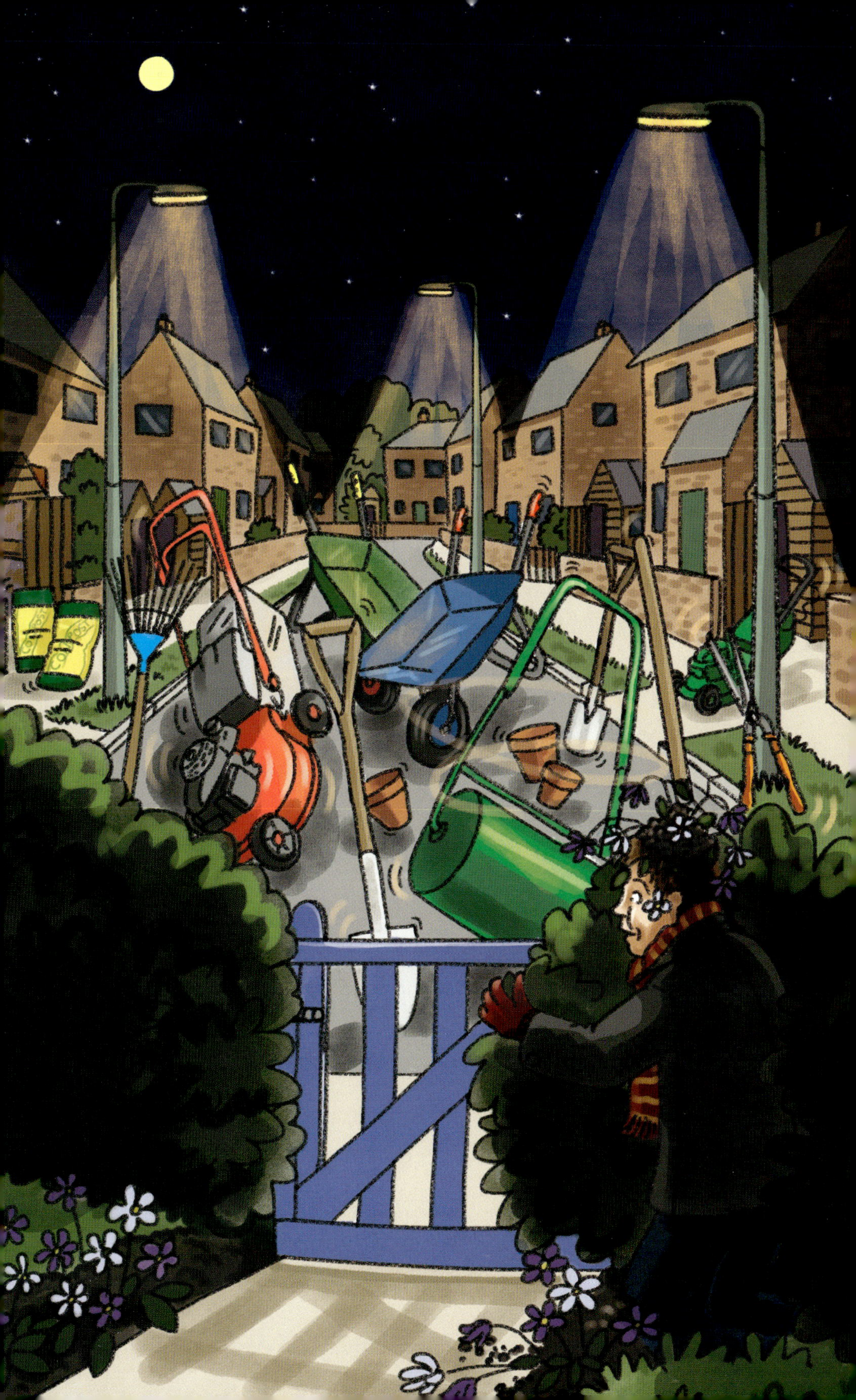

What was this partying all about?
Before I left, I found that out!
I overheard the spade and fork –
Yes, garden tools can actually talk!
I heard them say they missed the Spring
And all the work the season brings
That they were lonely in their shed
And longing to be used instead
But their owners locked them all away
All Winter long, all night and day
Gathering dust, with nothing to do
Confined by their too long curfew
So now I understood their plight
Why they escape each Winter's night
They yearn to work the flower beds
Hence their escape from garden sheds
They need a short break out of their 'jail'
So they grant themselves a kind of bail
They let off steam and dance with pride
Just half an hour then back inside
So no one sees their fun and games
I found it odd though all the same!
So when Spring finally comes around
And your parents want to dig the ground
And they open up their garden shed
And can't find their spade and scratch their head
Don't let their temperament explode
It just might have 're-homed' across the road!

Limerick

There once was a man from Surrey
Who went for a Vindaloo curry
He bought three on the trot
And scoffed down the lot
Then he needed the loo in a hurry!

'Twas the Night Before Christmas

'twas the night before Christmas
When all through the house
Nothing was stirring
Not even a mouse

Then all of a sudden
The house alarm sounded
Blue lights, police
and truncheons abounded

The police shone their torches
At the house cold and dark
Which caused a moggy to screech
And a dog loudly bark

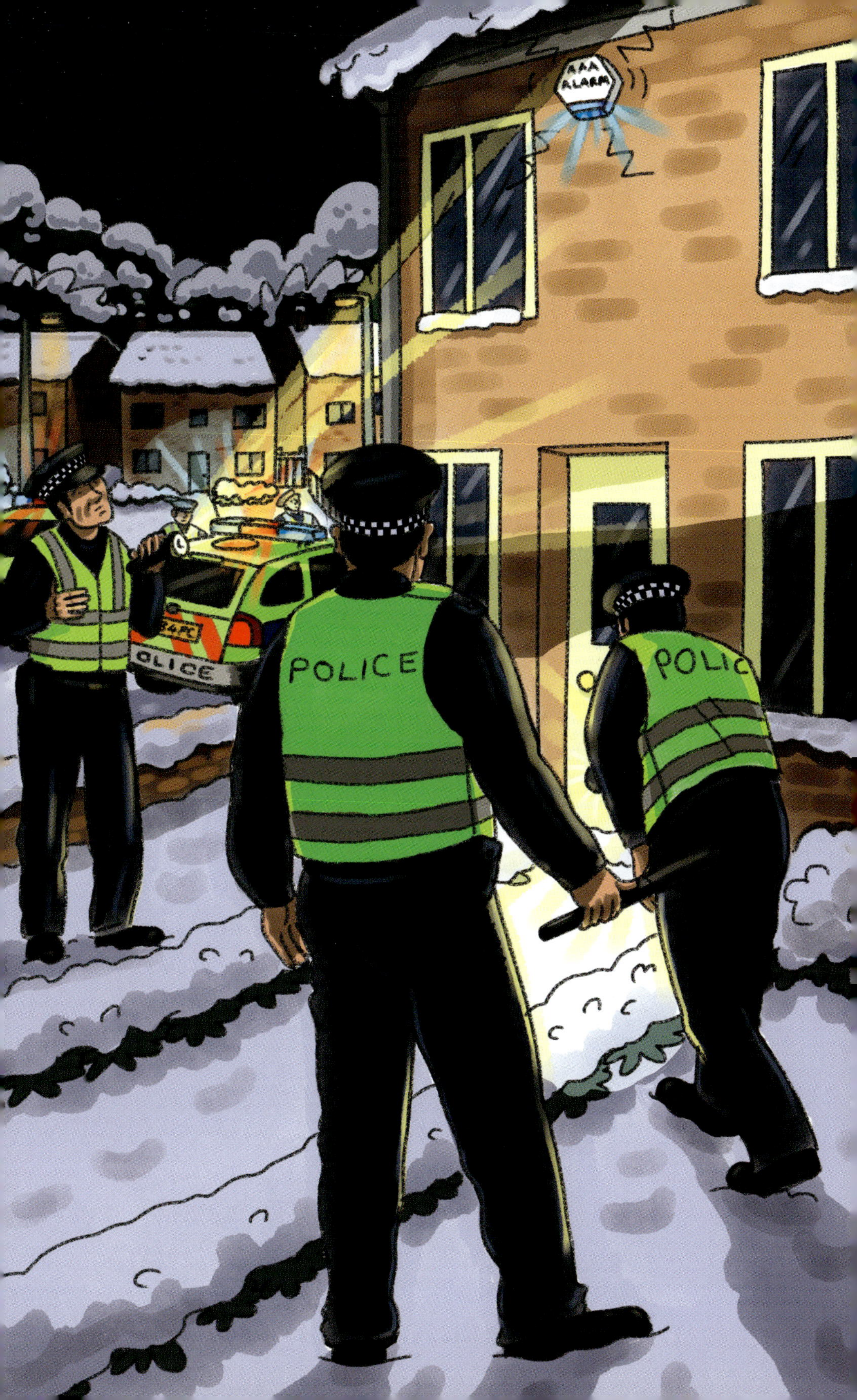
AAA ALARM
POLICE
POLIC
OLICE

They tiptoed on snow
Around the outside
Listening and checking
Their eyes open wide

The police couldn't see
Any robbers about
But just to ensure
They gave a window a clout

Then they let themselves in
And searched every space
Every room, every crevice
There was nought out of place

They were puzzled and baffled
As to what could have triggered
The intruder alarm –
It just had them jiggered!

But then they spotted their culprit
As bold as brass sat
Not an unsavoury criminal
But a big ugly RAT!

For there he was happily
Chewing with glee
The burglar alarm wires
As plain as could be

And hence the short circuit
Had set off the sounder
And all hell had broke loose
Because of this little bounder!

They chased the rodent outside
And repaired the alarm
Then returned to their homes
In the still and the calm

And after all of that bother
Would you believe
It was still the night before Christmas
T'was still Christmas Eve!

Then… a faint tinkling of bells
And a soft galloping of hooves
Could it be that Santa Claus man
Sledging over our roofs?

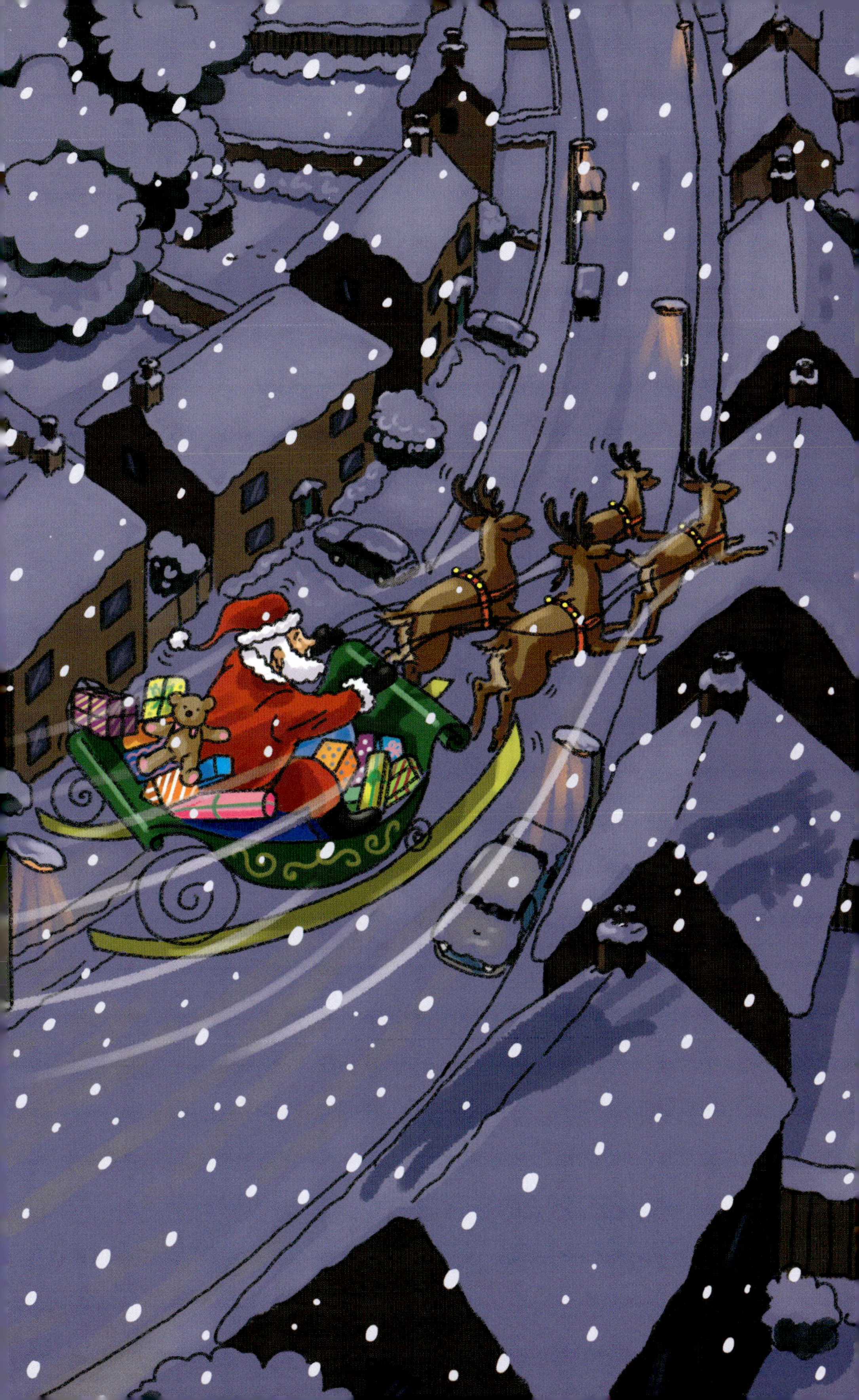

Jack Sprat

Jack Sprat could eat no fat
His wife could eat no beef
They only ate lamb
And boiled ham
And they ate it without any teeth!

Limerick

Old Mother Hubbard
Went to her cupboard
To fetch her fat doggy a bone
She banged her head
And dropped down dead
And the doggy soon lost half a stone!

Postman – No Pat!

My name is Pete the Postman
And I am standing at the gate
Of No.9 Elm Avenue
– A delivery I used to hate!

You see they have a pit bull terrier
And we did not see eye-to-eye
We had never been on friendly terms
And I often wondered why

Last week it chased me down the path
Whilst snarling wild at me
I managed to jump o'er the gate
And dislocate my knee!

It's always in the garden
Standing there 'on guard'
I'd always yearned to boot it
Halfway up the yard!

I'd tried to coax him to me
With a doggy biscuit treat
But it would start its fearful growling
And I would leg it up the street!

One day the owner stood there
And he waved me on, 'Do come'
I did and the beast jumped up
And bit me on the bum!

It sunk its teeth in both my legs
And once my arm required stitches
It's ravaged half my uniform
Especially my breeches!

So yesterday I waited at the gate
Then took hold of a brick
Slipped it in my letter-sack
And I had to do it quick

As it snarled and bared its teeth at me
I bravely walked up to the door
And as the dog began to pounce
I whacked it to the floor!

I got a bulls eye on its backside
And it let out a yelping whine
But I was pleased I'd taught a lesson
To the wretched little swine!

The owner is now mystified
Why I no longer fear or dread
This once psychopathic canine
Which I can now pat on the head!

Limerick

The Queen was about to bestow
A knighthood on a revered Eskimo
As he bowed down his head
She stabbed him instead
But he bled not of blood but of snow!

Miriam the Mouse

Miriam the mouse
Was left in the house
Whilst the owners went out for the day
She liked it like this
But her nemesis
Felix the cat, was in the way!
Miriam scratched her head
As she lay on the bed
Wondering what mischief to cause
Now the owners were out
She could wander about
But well away from those catty-wat paws!

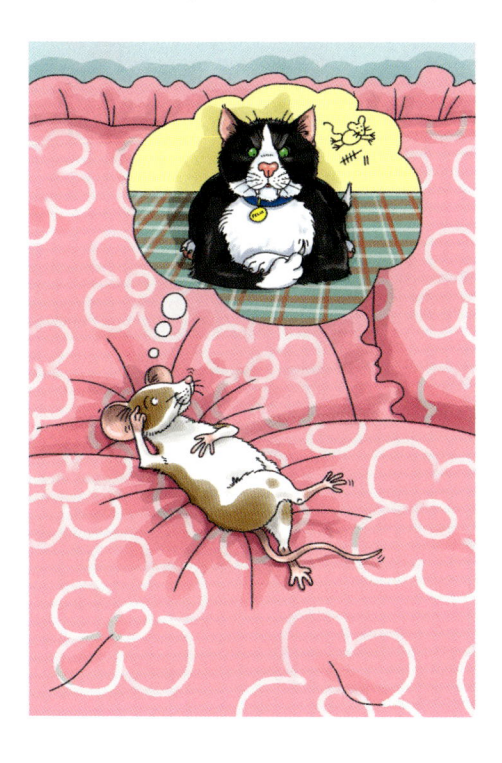

For Felix the cat
Was monstrously fat
And renowned for his slaughter of mice
He could pounce and kill
With effortless skill
No, Felix was not very nice!

Miriam tiptoed downstairs
With her family in pairs
Husband Joe, Pip and Polly, their twins
They kicked up such a palaver
As they whizzed past the larder
To food bulging from the waste bins

There were chocolates and sweets
And all manner of treats
Mouldy cheese, fruit cake, stale bread
Some sweet creamy rice
And all things that taste nice
Broken biscuits and marmalade spread

They filled up their bellies
'Til they wobbled like jellies
Then all of a sudden a big clatter
Appeared from the door
They waited some more
Undecided to hide or just scatter

It was that demon Felix for sure
As they peeped 'round the door
Was this how they'd now meet their fate?
They all trembled and quivered
And the little ones shivered
For fear of ending up on his plate!

Then they espied a large Hoover
And they had to manoeuvre
To flick on its switch at the socket
The noise made Felix wail
As it sucked up his tail
And then it blew up with the noise of a rocket!

He lay there concussed
The poor overweight puss
But the mice could now run for their nest
They had a near deathly scrape
But a lucky escape
And now needed a *mice* well-earned rest!

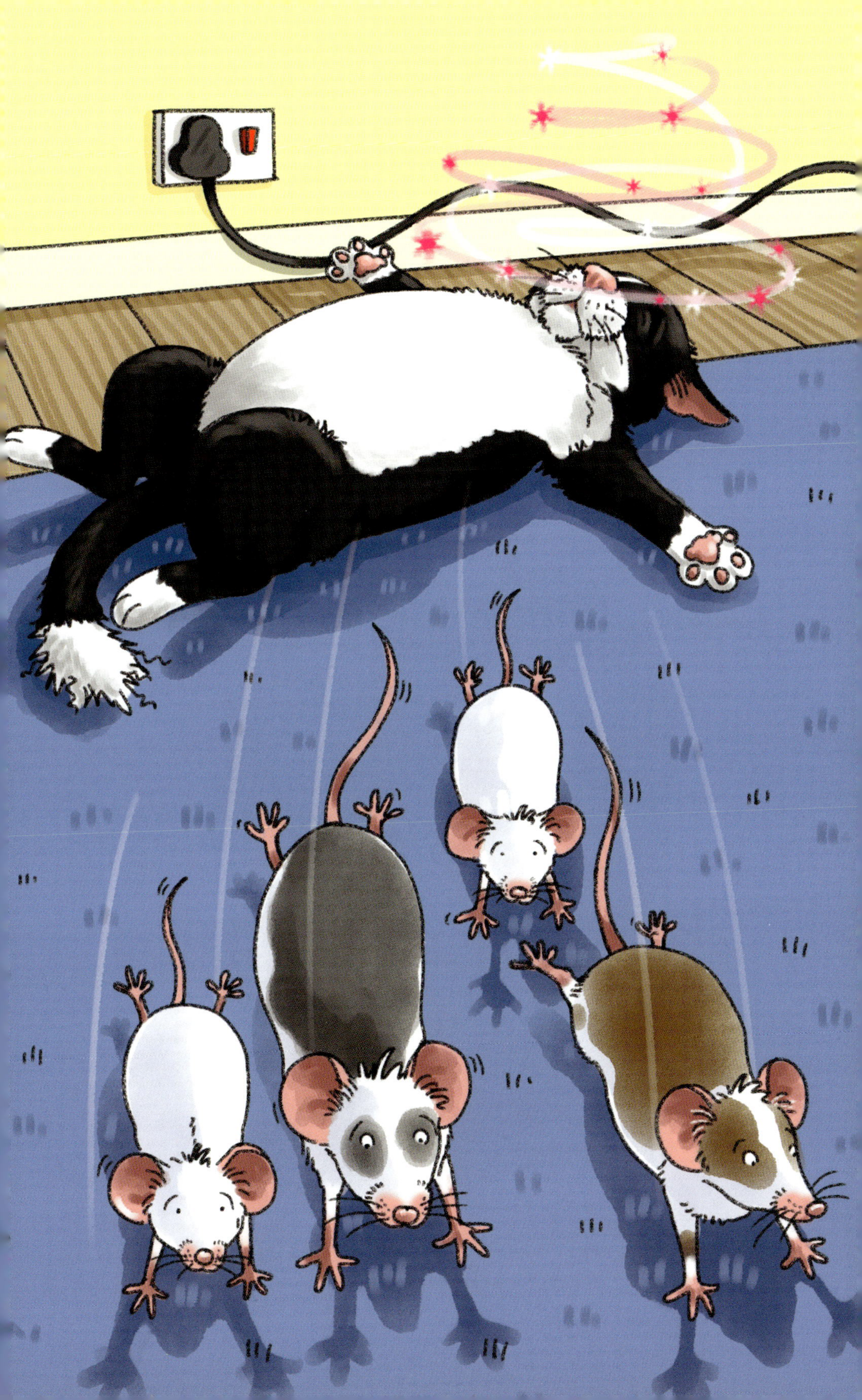

Limerick

A man engulfed by thick fog
Was walking one night with his dog
The fog was so dense
He did not have the sense
To go home and thus fell down a bog!

Limerick

Little Miss Muffet sat on a tuffet
Eating some ice cream and jelly
Along came a spider
Who sat down beside her
And together they both watched the telly

The Hungry Caterpillar

In the garden all was quiet
Then a munching sound that caused a riot
So loud the noise the birds all flew
The rabbits, squirrels scarpered too!
The ground it shook, the tree tops quivered
The badgers in their dark setts shivered
The noise was like a clap of thunder
We stood aghast in awe and wonder
There it was in bright sunlight
A furry, wriggly horrid sight!
It was bigger than a horse or cow
To have reached this size we know not how
It decimated my rows of veg
Like a steamroller mowing down a hedge

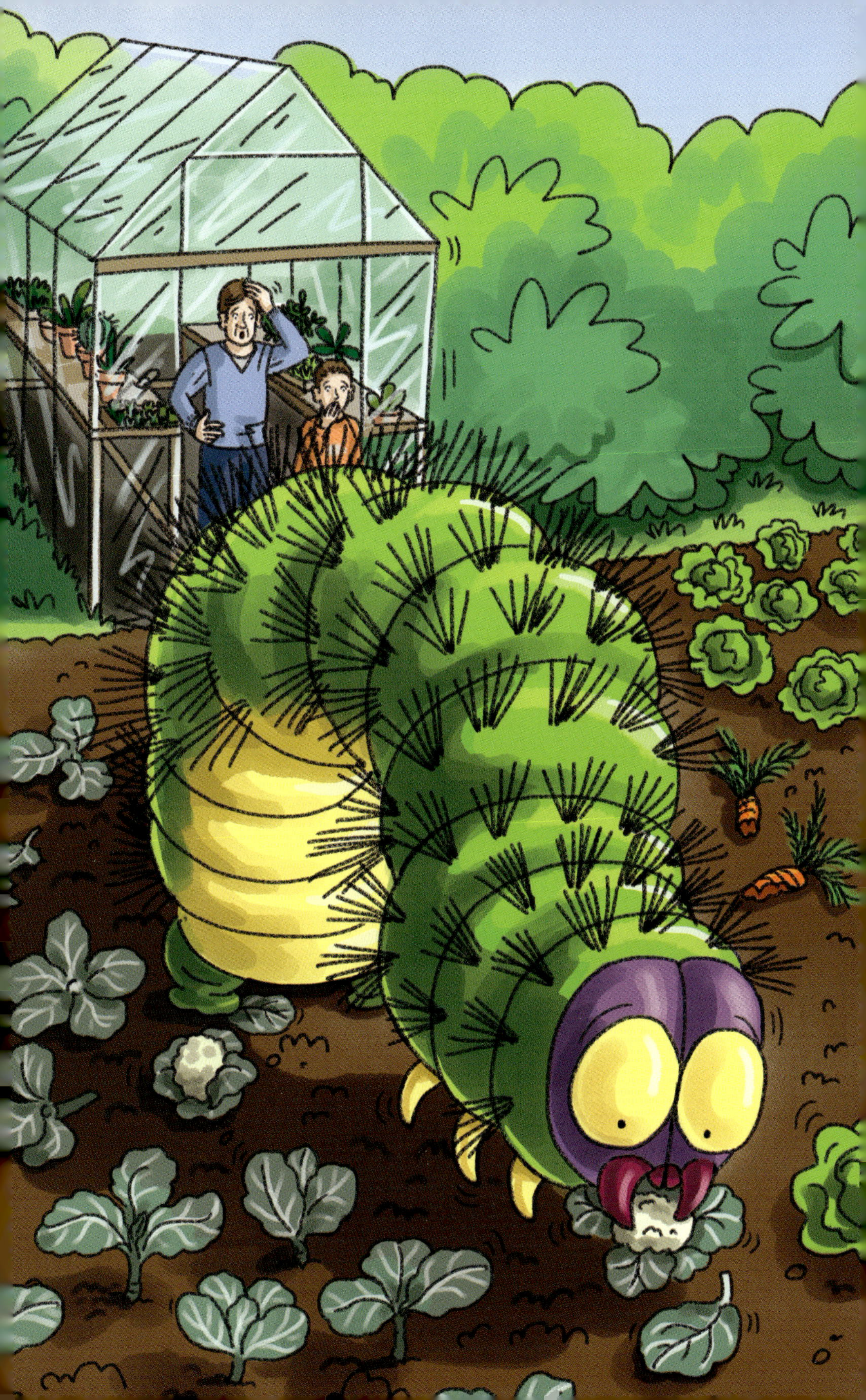

We watched it relentlessly devour
My turnips, beets and cauliflower
It even crushed my wheelbarrow
To gobble up my prize marrow
The lettuce, carrots, kale and peas
It gorged the cabbages with ease
All gone and not a bean was left!
Naturally, we were bereft
But the problem was to block its path
And encounter possibly its wrath
The only thing to be done
Was dial 999 and then to RUN!

Megan and Macy

Megan and Macy sat in a hutch
Two little brown rabbits – not loved very much
In a pet shop they sat all day and all night
Hoping someone might buy them if the price was alright
They were born as sisters – together since birth
They shared many a moment of laughter and mirth
Then one day the cage opened and in came a hand
Little Macy was taken but she did not understand

The customer wanted to buy just the one
So Megan was left and Macy was gone!
Megan scuttled in the cage in panic and fright
Little Macy was gone – and was long out of sight
Then later that day Megan also was bought
The hand reappeared and she likewise was caught
So Megan and Macy both now broken-hearted
Had been relocated and were forever now parted
They sat in their new homes all forlorn and sad
They pined for each other – they thought they'd go mad
Then with their heads pointed up to the sky
Their noses twitched frantically – but only they knew why!
They were using some extrasensory skill
But they had to concentrate hard and keep perfectly still

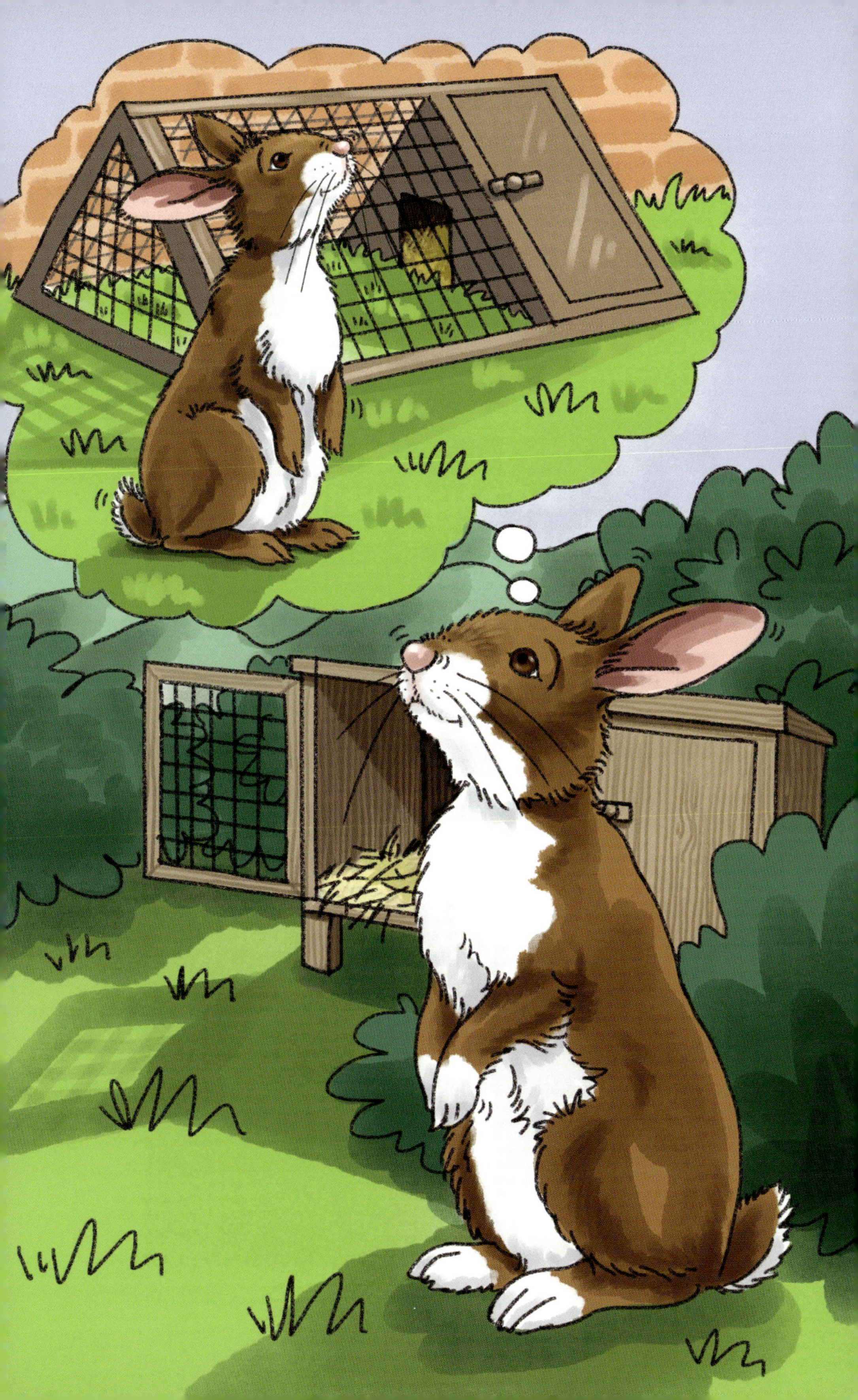

Then Eureka! They found it! A familiar scent
So fragrant, so recognisable, sheer wonderment!
So at the same hour, on the very next day
They both escaped from their new homes and scurried away
They started to dig into the ground a big hole
They furrowed and burrowed like a dynamic mole

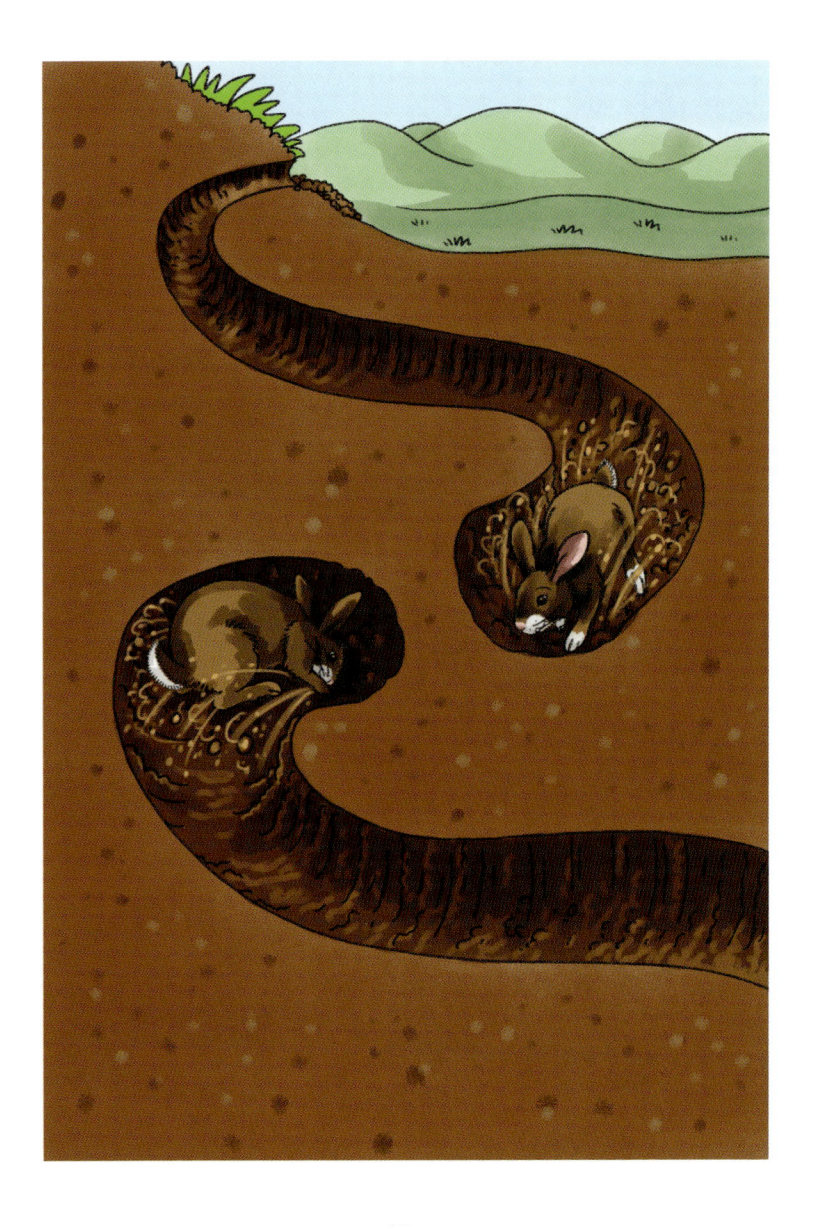

They dug and they tunnelled and some miles they did cover
In the desperate hope that they would find one another
Eventually success, the two tunnels converged
And their two little heads eventually emerged
They hugged and embraced and were filled with elation
And exchanged horror stories of their separation
They did a cute dance and a little bunny hop
And vowed they would never return to the pet shop
Instead they hopped off together, arm in arm, as they smiled
They would spend the rest of their days living out in the wild.

Sophie Wilson

Christmas Eve had arrived and excitement was high
But sweet Sophie Wilson just wanted to cry
For years she had yearned for a horse of her own
Not a laptop or Xbox or a smart mobile phone

But she knew that her parents did not have the resources
To go wasting good money on extravagant horses!
So when she awoke there at the foot of the bed
There was no horse to be seen but a bucket instead…

With a trail of oats leading out of the door
Sophie followed it curiously – what could this be for?
She followed it downstairs through the kitchen, the hall
Out through the backyard and over a wall
Then there in a field this fine equine beast stood
With fine shoulders and withers and thoroughbred blood

So sweet Sophie's dreams were clearly not shattered
Owning this horse was all that now mattered
He was a stallion called Blaze, as white as the snow
She couldn't wait to find out how fast he would go!
She climbed on his back and stroked his soft mane
Patted his neck and tugged on the rein
She dug her heels in his side and he took off at pace
She had the wind in her hair and the sun on her face
They galloped through buttercup fields at a rate
Then too suddenly before them appeared a large gate
Blaze reared up on his hind legs such that Sophie slid off
With her bum in the air and her nose in a trough!

She screamed out so loud from her fall off the horse
That she woke up in bed – she'd been dreaming of course!

Icky Wicky Woo

Icky Wicky Woo
The witch mixes her brew
Greeny, yellowy, murky slime
A can of snails, a heap of grime
A cup of spiders, an ounce of fat
A bit of this, a lump of that
A scoop of flies
A bowl of bees
A pinch of moths
A cup of fleas
The blood of rats
Including tails
The clippings of her
Finger nails!
Her toothless grin
Her evil eye
Her matted hair
To terrify

Everyone who ventures near
She'll cast a spell – have no fear
To toss you in her stewing pot
Slimy, greeny, bubbling hot!
Ooh no thanks, I'd rather not!

The Loch Ness Monster

We travelled up to Scotland
In the hope that we might see
The famous Loch Ness Monster
But there was no guarantee

Many folk had gone before us
To catch a glance or peep
But none had ever witnessed
The so-called monster of the deep

We made camp on the south shore
Our log fire gently glimmered
The sky was black as coal dust
The moon on the water shimmered

We sat, we watched, we waited
Not a ripple or a splash
If we'd seen any kind of movement
We'd have been on it like a flash

It was misty, cold and silent
A damp and moonlit night
But not a stirring in the water
And no Nessie in our sight!

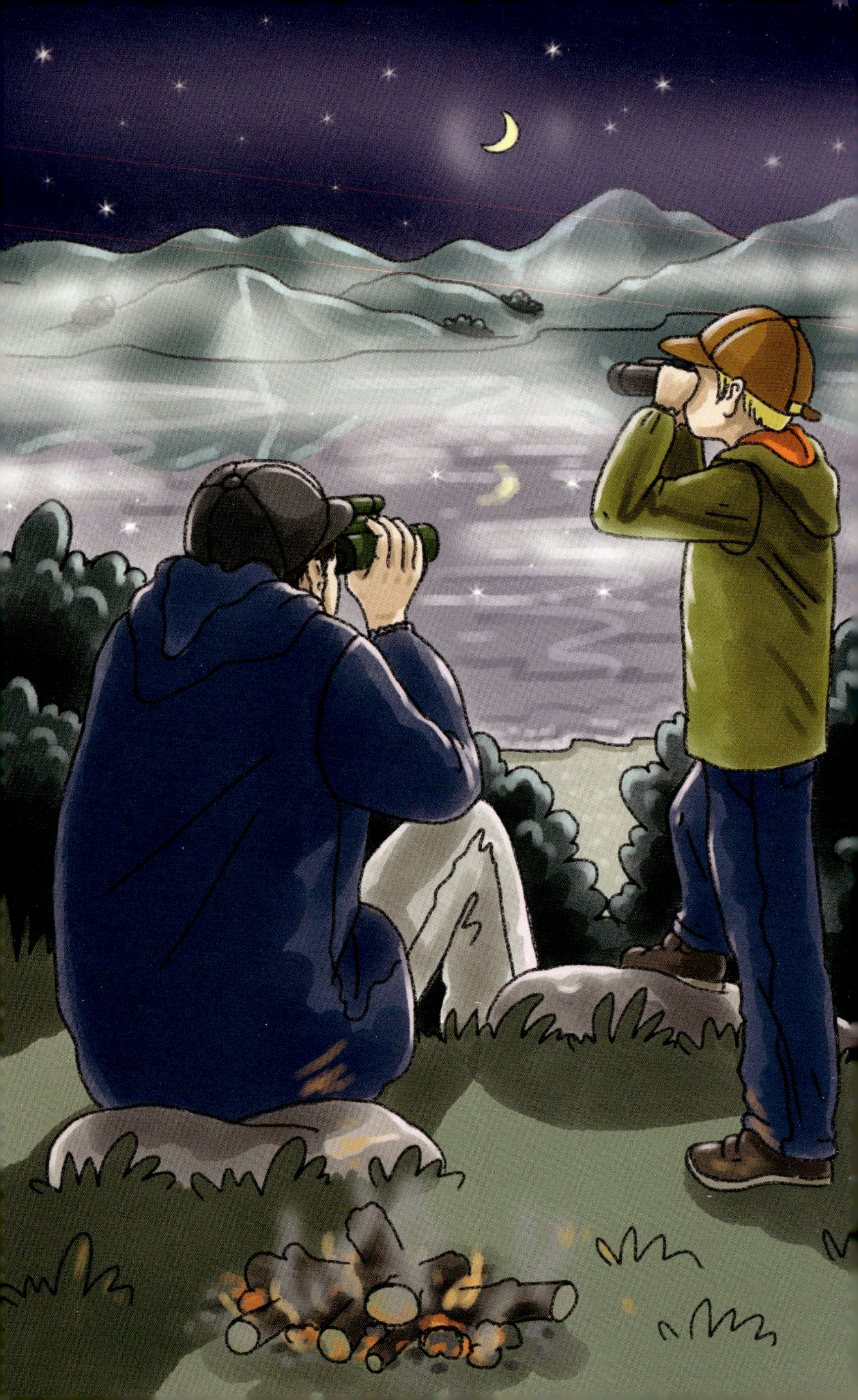

The vigil was soon over
We were breakfasting at dawn
Bleary-eyed from lack of sleep
And now feeling quite forlorn

Five nights did this continue
Five nights of cold damp air
Peering through binoculars
But lo – she was not there!

So the last night in desperation
We took an old wooden boat
Rowed out into the water
And prayed we'd stay afloat

Then *thud* something had hit us
And filled with horror and despair
We peeked over the side to see
We'd been scooped up in mid-air!

It was the Loch Ness Monster!
We were balanced on her tail!
She skimmed across the water
With the poise of a blue whale

We clung on tightly to the boat
As Nessie took us back to shore
Where she dumped us unceremoniously
And was gone and seen no more!

We stood aghast – in sheer amazement!
We'd had our moment of true glory
A ride on the Loch Ness Monster
But who would believe our story!

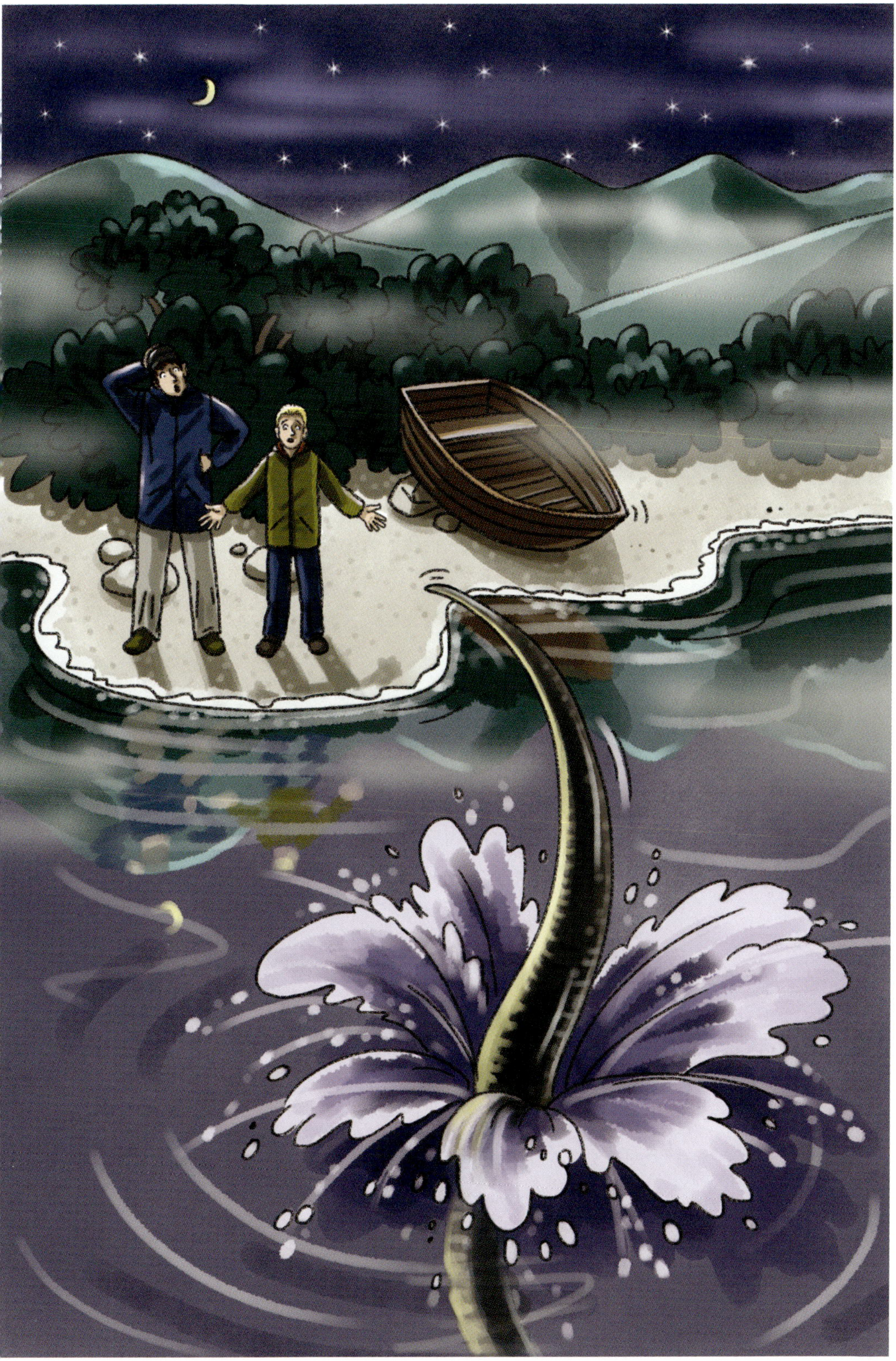

Lulu Letterbox

My name is Lulu Letterbox
I live out on the street
I wear a mostly red, long dress
But I have no hands or feet

People feed me envelopes
Of every shape and size
The coloured ones taste yummiest
But plastic I despise

When my tummy's filled up
And no more letters I can swallow
A smiling postman empties me
And once again I'm hollow

My prized letters are the pinky ones
They have a distinct flavour
They are smooth and creamy textured
And are the ones I like to savour

I have lots of family members
Who are letterboxes too
If we all huddled together
You couldn't tell who was who

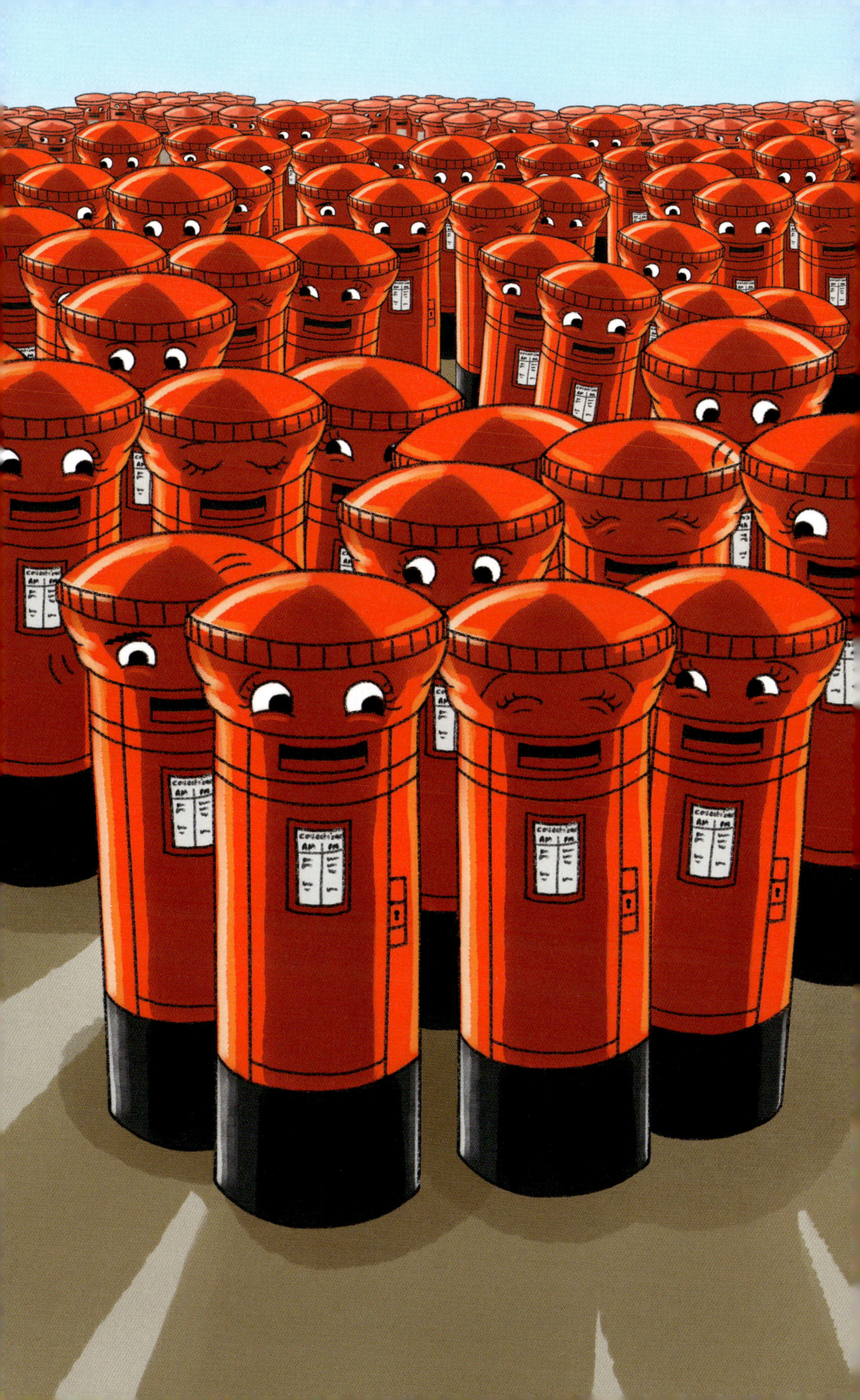

But one thing is for certain
We all love letters with a stamp
Some are thick or wafer-thin
And when it's raining, some are damp!

So next time you post a letter
Give me a pat or just say, 'Hi!'
Don't think me just a letterbox
And politely pass me by!

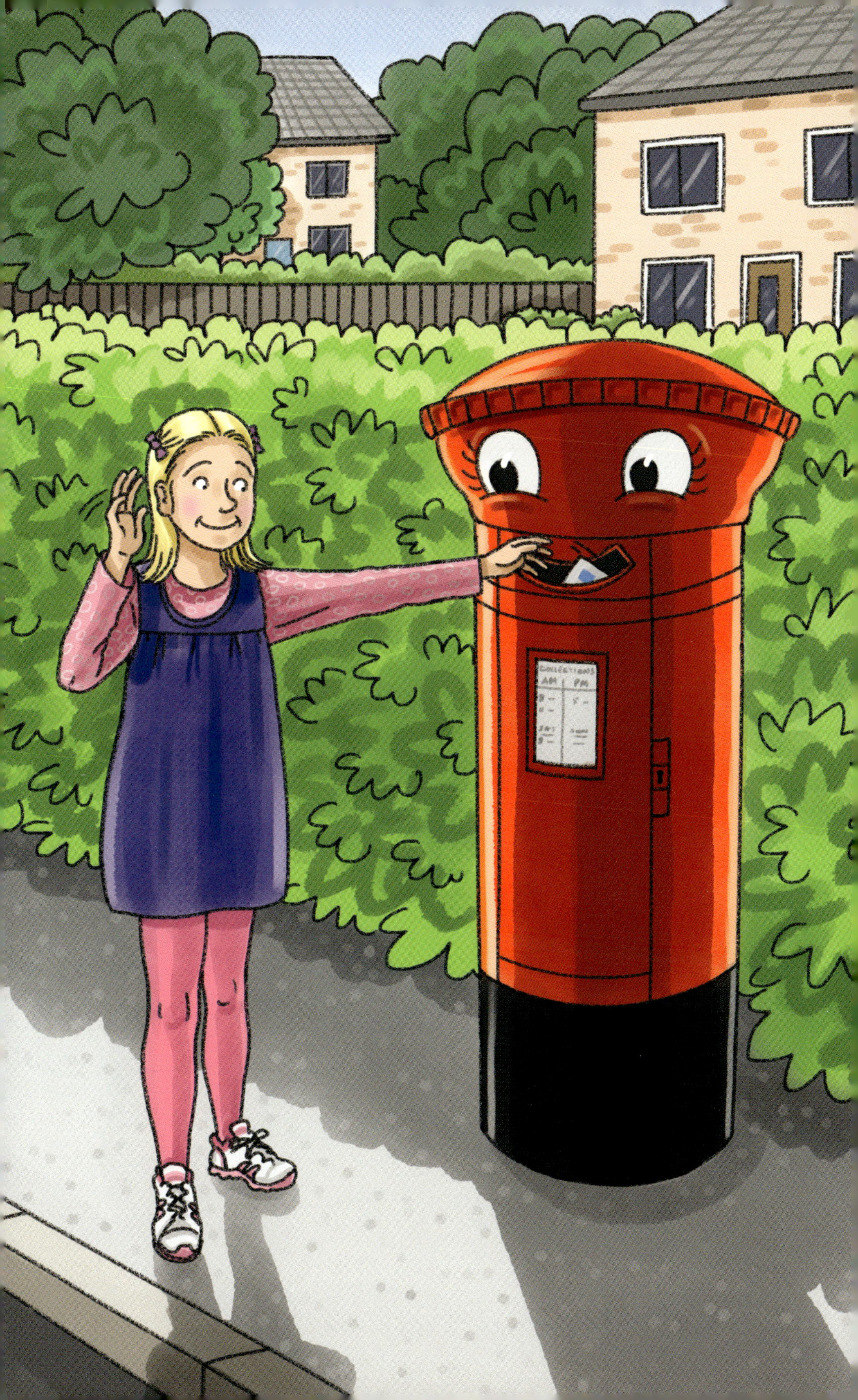
COLLECTIONS
AM
PM

Acknowledgements

I would like to express my sincere gratitude to Punch Limited for allowing me to include in my book the adaptation to the Patrick Barrington poem 'I Had a Hippopotamus' published 21st June 1933 in *Punch* magazine.